WRITING A POSITION PAPER

FOR HISTORY STUDENTS

By Mark B. Wilson
Lehman College, City University of New York

Writing a Position Paper for History Students
by Mark B. Wilson

ISBN-13: 978-1479103638
ISBN-10: 1479103632

http://markbwilson.com
mark@markbwilson.com

CONTENTS

Writing a strong, effective position paper means taking a position and using evidence to convince your reader. You will find that the skills involved in planning, structuring, and executing a strong, effective position paper will be useful to you not only in other academic assignments, but in any situation in which you want someone else to believe something.

The purpose of this book is to provide a concise guide to framing a position paper that effectively argues an interesting assessment of some key moment in human history.

STEP ONE: PROBLEM AND THESIS

The most important component of your paper is the position you want to convince your reader of. In a position paper, this takes the form of **the thesis**: a sentence at the end of your introductory paragraph that states an opinion that someone could disagree with, which you will then seek to prove in the body of your paper.

The Problem

One way of looking at a thesis is as the answer to a problem— something about a time and place that seems to need explaining. This can be phrased as a question. But it's important to take a close look at your question and see whether it will work for your paper. You need to test your question in two ways: (a) are there two or more sides historians might argue, and (b) is the scope too big or too small for the paper I am writing?

For example, if you're interested in Hannibal's war with Rome, you might first want to look at the big question: "Why did Hannibal lose?" This is a good one in terms of the first test, because historians have given lots of conflicting answers over the last 2200 y`ears. But it's also huge, which might mean you'll be in trouble on the second test.

In this case you'd want to narrow it down to a more specific question about Hannibal's war that still has different possible answers, like "Why didn't Hannibal attack Rome?" or "Did Hannibal's elephants really make a difference?"

The first test—are there different answers?—is crucial. If your question were something like "Why did Hannibal attack Rome?" you could write a long paper answering it, but it wouldn't be a position paper because there's really no disagreement: Rome was Carthage's economic nemesis; their expanding interests created inevitable conflict, leading to a previous war—one result of which was Hannibal being raised to despise the Romans. Unless you've unearthed some radical, game-changing new evidence, it would be very hard to imagine two sides to this question.

That's why I recommend that your introduction include a statement of the problem, followed by statements that might be made by historians arguing different, opposing answers. You should be able to express these competing ideas in a **"some say... others say..."** formula, even if you don't use those actual words.

For example, here's the start of a sample introduction:

> Hannibal Barca, the great Carthaginian general, brought 37 war elephants with him over the Alps into Italy, and at the climactic Battle of Zama he had a front line that included 80 elephants. Did Hannibal's elephants really make a difference? Some say that Hannibal's elephants were crucial in establishing the morale of his troops against the legendary Roman legions and in intimidating other armies along the way into alliances; but others say that Hannibal's elephants did the Carthaginian side more harm than good in their fight with Rome.

Here the introduction is shown with three of its four important elements: setting, problem, and possible positions. The fourth element needed for the introduction is the thesis.

The Thesis

Your thesis, then, must provide *your answer* to the problem or question you've posed. If your problem meets the two tests—it has two or more possible positions and it has a manageable scope—then your thesis should easily meet the main requirement, which is that it must be a **statement of opinion that someone could disagree with**.

That's why something like "Hannibal Barca was a Carthaginian general" would make a bad thesis. There's no conflict, there's no possible disagreement. No one would want to read a paper attempting to prove this.

In fact the rule here is to go as far as possible in the other direction. **The more radical, the better**—as long as you have evidence to back it up. (More on evidence in a moment.) For example, a thesis like "Hannibal was really an extraterrestrial from the planet Mondegreen" is a wonderful thesis. Everyone would want to read the paper trying to prove this thesis—which is where the whole supporting evidence thing comes in.

The best thesis is one that states a position, *and* gives an extremely concise summary of the "reasons why" that you're going to give. You should be able to express your thesis using the formula **"I believe... because..."**.

For example, here's a thesis statement that might complete the partial sample introduction quoted above:

> I believe that Hannibal's use of elephants was a mistake,
> not because war elephants were a dumb idea in general,
> but because Roman adaptability meant that they would
> inevitably find a way around them.

This thesis not only sets out what you're going to prove in your paper, but gives you the magic number of topics to cover in the body of your paper—three. Using your thesis as a guideline, you know you'll need sections on (a) why war elephants could be effective in ancient battle scenarios; (b) adaptability as a key and intrinsic trait for the Romans, especially in war; and (c) how that adaptability ended up trumping the usefulness of elephants when the Carthaginians faces the

Romans. Now you just need to assemble, and discuss, the evidence available in each of these three areas.

Notice that you're supporting your thesis with three assertions that in themselves are statements of opinion—they are sort of mini-theses. This logical structure is why a position paper works to convince the reader. Your thesis rests on opinions A, B, and C. You can prove A easily using evidence. You can prove B, too, with the evidence related to that assertion. And then C flows naturally from A and B, brought home using the evidence related to C. Demonstrating that A, B, and C are true convinces your reader that your thesis is true, too.

A good thesis, in other words, provides you with the skeleton for the body of your paper.

Here's the sample introduction in full:

> Hannibal Barca, the great Carthaginian general, brought 37 war elephants with him over the Alps into Italy, and at the climactic Battle of Zama he had a front line that included 80 elephants. Did Hannibal's elephants really make a difference? Some say that Hannibal's elephants were crucial in establishing the morale of his troops against the legendary Roman legions and in intimidating other armies along the way into alliances; but others say that Hannibal's elephants did the Carthaginian side more harm than good in their fight with Rome. I believe that Hannibal's use of elephants was a mistake, not because war elephants were a dumb idea in general, but because Roman adaptability meant that they would inevitably find a way around them.

Now you've not only told the reader what you're going to demonstrate, but you've also given yourself a road map of how you're going to set about doing it.

STEP TWO: EVIDENCE AND ANALYSIS

I said before that three "reasons why" your thesis is convincing is the magic number. You can think of them as pillars, because what they're doing is supporting your argument. Plenty of papers have been written with more than three pillars, and you might be able to support an argument (for some readers) with two or even one pillar. But long experience suggests that **three pillars** is the most sturdy and aesthetically effective way of supporting a thesis in a position paper like this one.

The body of your paper, then, will have three sections. Each starts with the assertion you hinted at in the thesis statement. Then you provide evidence supporting that assertion, and finally you interpret that evidence, showing the reader how it effectively illustrates the assertion, and so in turn supports your overall thesis.

What evidence do you need to assemble and describe? In most historical situations, you want to provide two kinds of evidence: (a) examples from the time and place that show what you asserted was what actually happened, and (b) expert testimony from scholars who have deeply studied the relevant events or texts. In other words, you ideally want to provide both primary sources and secondary sources.

For example, in my sample thesis the first topic—my first pillar— involves discussing why war elephants are not *normally* a bad idea, or, to put it another way, to show that the reason Hannibal's elephants were a mistake was *not* that elephants were a mistake in general, because what my paper is really about is Roman adaptability as the thing that threw a wrench in the works. So I need to show that war elephants were effective in other contexts—ideally, for the Carthaginians in other wars, if possible.

I can do that by providing examples of effective elephants from the ancient literature. For example, I could summarize primary sources that show Alexander of Macedon using elephants effectively at the Battle of the Hydaspes River, the Seleucids using elephants well at the Battle of Ipsus and against the Maccabees, and the Ptolemaic Egyptians at the battle of Raphia. (See the Rule of Threes surfacing again? Remember, each of your three sections is making its own argument that requires convincing your reader, so three pieces of evidence are ideal.)

Primary sources provide accounts or narratives of events; you next need to talk about *how and why* the elephants are effective. Here's where secondary works come in. In this case, you want scholars who specialize in either ancient military tactics or specifically in Macedonian-style warfare, talking about theory behind elephant warfare and why the ancients kept turning to it during this period.

The last paragraphs of this section are for your interpretation, where you make connections between your sources. Your interpretation shows how your sources demonstrate the assertion you're making in this section, and makes it clear that this helps support your overall thesis. You can't just throw the evidence at the reader: first describe it, then tell the reader what it means.

That means the structure of the paper so far is something like this:

I.   Introduction
    A. Context
    B. Question
    C. Possible positions   ("some say... others say...")
    D. Thesis statement   ("I believe... because...")

II.   Elephants were not a dumb idea in general
    A. Examples from primary sources
       1. Alexander
       2. Seleucids
       3. Ptolemaic Egyptians
    B. Expert opinion on effectiveness of elephant warfare
    C. My interpretation of what the evidence means and why it shows elephants were not a dumb idea

Sections III (Roman adaptability) and IV (How Roman adaptability trumped the effectiveness of elephants) will follow the same structure as section II. Finally, you'll end the paper with a conclusion that ties together the three sections of your main body, and show how they demonstrate the validity of your thesis statement.

FINDING EVIDENCE

Finding evidence for any given historical problem is easy. Finding the right evidence that will help you make a convincing argument is hard. Therefore, my rule of thumb is, start with the evidence that's easy to find, and let it point you toward the evidence that *it* relies on.

For example, it's often easier to find the secondary sources than the primary. But remember the definition of a secondary source: it's the work of a scholar *using primary sources* to provide his or her own interpretation of events.

So a scholarly secondary source is going to be based on primary sources—and the secondary source's text, footnotes, and bibliography will tell you which ones and where to look in them.

Finding Books

So, start by looking for books. Tertiary sources like textbooks and encyclopedias can help you here: just as secondary sources are based on primary sources and can point you toward them, tertiary sources are based on secondary sources and can point you toward them. A textbook on ancient history or ancient Rome will usually have a "Suggested readings" section for each chapter and/or a Bibliography; these will give you the names of books that you might want to try to find. History-related articles in online encyclopedias, while notoriously unreliable, normally have a sources section that lists relevant books on the subject.

(Remember: tertiary sources cannot be used as sources of evidence in your paper. This includes textbooks, encyclopedias, and almost everything on the web apart from online scholarly journals.)

If there's a book that's obviously useful—say you've come across references to the book *War Elephants* by John Kistler—the next step is to try to get that book through the library system by looking up the book title in the online catalog.

Some university systems allow you to access books even if they're not at the campus you're attending. For example, the Kistler book is not at the Lehman College library—but it is at John Jay College, which is within the CUNY system. The CUNY libraries' online catalog allows you to click on the "Request" button, and within a few days the librarians at John Jay College will have sent it to Lehman for you to borrow.

If the book weren't in the university system at all, you'd still have the option to have it sent to you through an online Interlibrary Loan request: if it's at another regional library you'll get it delivered via ILL in a week or two.

Another option would be to check the book's availability at the NYPL, using the online catalog at http://catalog.nypl.org. If it's at the main library on Fifth Avenue (and many, many books that aren't available elsewhere are available there), and it's essential to your paper, it might sense to plan an afternoon in midtown to make use of what you can find there. (You can't borrow books out from the reading room there, but you can photocopy important pages and take notes.)

Another tactic is browsing the topic. Start by searching the online catalog for relevant keywords: *ancient war, Roman wars, elephants, Hannibal, Zama*, etc. As you do these searches take note of the call numbers for books that seem like they might be useful. The call numbers will start to cluster in two or three different areas.

For example, Roman military history is around DG89 (history—ancient Italy—armies), but also U35 (military science—Rome). Books on Hannibal will be in DG249 (history—ancient Italy—Second Punic War). *War Elephants*, the book I noted above, is at UH87 (military science—other). And so on.

So here's the big trick: Once you find the call number clusters, **go and look at the shelf** for each of them and see what's *next to* the books that came up in your search. Because every time I do research, the book that's most useful to me is **on the shelf next to the books that came up in the catalog search.**

Take down books with likely titles—and, before you even carry them to your table, check two things: the Table of Contents and the Index. They'll tell you if that book covers subjects that will be useful to you and your thesis. If you've got a book on Hannibal in your hand, but the index doesn't list elephants, you can confidently put it back—it won't help you with this paper.

Once you have a book in hand, you can harvest *its* sources by checking the footnotes and bibliography for (a) mentions of other secondary sources that seem to be the seminal books in the field and (b) important primary sources and the relevant passages in them. So a book on the Second Punic War will often mention both the most important scholarly books on that war, some of which you'll want to try to find. It will also refer not only to the primary source authors who wrote about that war, but it will specify the crucial passages in those works.

In this way, using what you have, you can assemble what you need.

Finding Journal Articles

In addition to scholarly books, you'll want to look for another kind of secondary source: journal articles. Books are generally comprehensive approaches to a general subject, with titles like *Hannibal* or *The Second Punic War* or *War Elephants*. Journal articles are much more narrow and circumscribed. Like a position paper, journal articles are usually written to answer a very specific question.

Most of the classics and history journals are archived in JSTOR, an online database, available through most university library web sites, where you can (a) search by keywords and authors, and (b) retrieve full-text PDFs of the articles.

For example, a JSTOR search reveals that there is a journal article called "*Magister Elephantorvm*: A Reappraisal of Hannibal's Use of Elephants" by Michael B. Charles and Peter Rhodan that argues that Hannibal's use of elephants at Zama illustrates his tendency to take risks in battle; and another by Charles, "African Forest Elephants and Turrets in the Ancient World," that takes on the very particular and contentious question of whether ancient warfare with the small African forest elephants involved the use of turrets, or howdahs.

From searches like these you can find a wealth of information. You may find articles that are spot on for your subject, and will be directly useful both (a) as expert secondary evidence you can quote or summarize in your paper, and (b) as directories of the most important classical and secondary sources on the subject. (Charles and Rhodan's copious footnotes cite every important book, article, and classical source on Hannibal and elephants.)

Even without articles that perfectly intersect with your thesis, just the search and a glimpse at the resulting articles, even the ones that aren't exactly what you need, give you useful information—like who's writing about these subjects (apparently Prof. Charles is one of the experts on ancient war elephants) and what the burning issues are in this field.

You can also use JSTOR to find a particular article referenced elsewhere. For example, you might have come across a footnote citing the Charles and Rhodan article in a book you've found; you could then look for the article in JSTOR.

Finally, a JSTOR search may return book reviews of books that might be helpful; you can then go and find that book. For example, my JSTOR search on the keywords "*war elephants hannibal*" turned up a review of a book called *Hannibal's Elephants* by Alfred Powers; that book might have been worth investigating.

(Do not use just the review as a source. The reviewer will have picked only the elements of the book that stood out to him to write about, making the review both a subjective and an incomplete treatment of the material covered in the book.)

TELL 'EM WHAT YOU JUST TOLD 'EM

The final section of your paper summarizes the arguments made in the paper and connects them, showing how they support the thesis you made at the beginning.

Counterarguments

To make your position as convincing as possible, one thing you'll want to consider is: What would someone say if they wanted to disagree with you? The reason this is important is that your reader may remain unconvinced because you haven't dealt with an objection he or she already knows about and is mentally setting against your arguments. Your paper is not effective because you haven't countered the opposing argument.

Suppose you were writing a paper that said that Louis XIV was a great king who made France stronger. Anyone familiar with French history, reading your paper, might be thinking, "Yeah, well, what about revoking the Edict of Nantes? Exiling the artisan and middle-class Protestants was a huge and long-lasting blow to the French economy, wasn't it?" Your argument and your evidence might be well structured and impressively interpreted, but your reader may still set down your paper unsatisfied, still thinking to herself, "But what about the Edict of Nantes?"

So before you begin your conclusion paragraph, consider a paragraph where you address what an opponent in a debate, for example, might say to rebut you after you've had your say. You should be able to phrase this paragraph using a formula like **"Some might say... . In fact, however, ..."**. In this example, you want to show why revoking the Edict doesn't tarnish Louis XIV, either because the impact wasn't that major or because the other things Louis did outweighed it in benefiting France in the ways you've previously described.

CITATIONS: FOOTNOTES & BIBLIOGRAPHIES

Citations are absolutely essential in any academic paper, but particularly and especially in history. All information that is not from your own head must be cited, whether it's a direct quote, a paraphrase, or even just an idea.

Citations are how we can tell the difference between what you're claiming is your research and analysis, and the work of others. If you don't cite others' work, you're claiming it for your own, and that's plagiarism. Plagiarism is not tolerated at any academic institution; the lightest you'll get off is a zero for the paper, but in many cases harsher penalties are invoked, including an F for the course and academic disciplinary proceedings that may result in a range of transcript-damaging punishments.

It is therefore crucial that you distinguish evidence you've gathered from primary and secondary sources from your own discussion, interpretation, and analysis. You do that with citations.

Consider the article by Charles and Rhodan I alluded to above. There are a number of ways that that article might crop up in your paper. You might have quoted it directly:

> It's clear that Roman adaptability rendered the power of elephants moot. "Scipio had the answer to the elephant question, and the Punic elephants, when they were not doing damage to Hannibal's own troops, were unable to inflict any real damage on the enemy infantry."

Or you could have paraphrased it:

> It's clear that Roman adaptability rendered the power of elephants moot. Scipio was ready for them, and Hannibal's elephants, even setting aside the injury they did to the Carthaginians, ended up not causing any real damage to the Romans.

Or you might have just used the idea the authors were putting forward:

> It's clear that Roman adaptability rendered the power of elephants moot. When Hannibal's elephants attacked, the Romans were ready for them.

All three of these assertions require a citation, because all of them derive not from your own head, but from Charles and Rhodan. Making these assertions in any form without acknowledging that you got them from Charles and Rhodan is plagiarism and deserves a failing grade.

The citation system in your paper has two components: the bibliography and the footnotes.

The Bibliography

The Bibliography goes at the very end of your paper. It is a list of all of the books and articles you used for the paper. Every book and article you used as source material must appear in the bibliography, once.

Each entry in the bibliography gives the reader all the information they need to find that book or article if they need to. For a book, you have to give

   (a) the author,
   (b) the year,
   (c) the title of the book, and
   (d) the city and name of the publisher.

For an article, you need to give

   (a) the author,
   (b) the year,
   (c) the title of the article,
   (d) the journal name,
   (e) the volume number, and
   (f) the pages within that volume that the article covers.

A bibliography listing all the books and articles referred to in this guidebook so far would look like this:

Charles, Michael B. 2008. "African Forest Elephants and Turrets in the Ancient World." *Phoenix* 62: 338–362.

Charles, Michael B. and Peter Rhodan. 2007. "*Magister Elephantorvm*: A Reappraisal of Hannibal's Use of Elephants." *The Classical World* 100: 363–389.

Kistler, John M. 2006. *War Elephants*. Westport, Conn: Praeger.

Powers, Alfred. 1944. *Hannibal's Elephants*. New York: Longmans & Co.

The bibliography is alphabetized by the authors' last names, and is not numbered.

Footnotes

I described the bibliography first because what footnotes do is **point to an entry in the bibliography.** For example, in the three sample uses of Charles and Rhodan described above, each of them needs a footnote after what comes from the article:

> It's clear that Roman adaptability rendered the power of elephants moot. "Scipio had the answer to the elephant question, and the Punic elephants, when they were not doing damage to Hannibal's own troops, were unable to inflict any real damage on the enemy infantry against which they had been arrayed."[1]

---

[1]Charles and Rhodan 2007, 388.

> It's clear that Roman adaptability rendered the power of elephants moot. Scipio was ready for them, and Hannibal's elephants, even setting aside the injury they did to the Carthaginians, ended up not causing any real damage to the Romans.[1]

---

[1]Charles and Rhodan 2007, 388.

> It's clear that Roman adaptability rendered the power of elephants moot. When Hannibal's elephants attacked at Zama, the Romans were ready for them.[1]

---

[1]Charles and Rhodan 2007, 388.

Note that each footnote is actually pointing to an item in your bibliography. In each case, a footnote gives two pieces of information: (a) **which book or article** and (b) **what page in that book or article**—that is, which page would a reader go to in order to find the information you've just referred to?

You can think of the relationship between the footnotes and the bibliography like so:

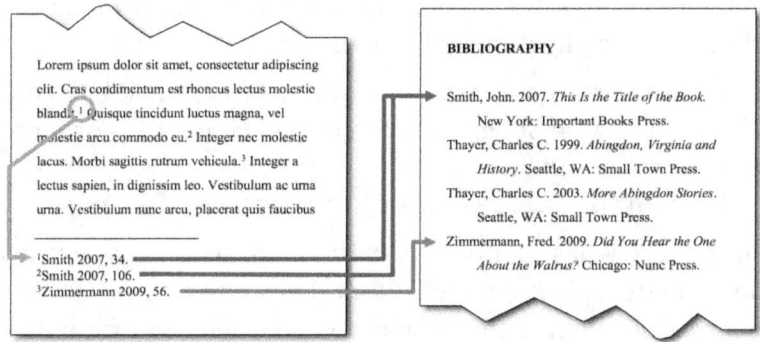

The first footnote in this illustration is shorthand for what you're really telling the reader: "You can find this information on page 34 of the book in my bibliography that's written by Smith and published in 2007."

Usually author plus year is enough to identify a particular work. If an author has written more than one book or article that you're using that was published in the same year, then the years are given in the bibliography as 1999a, 1999b, etc., and the book is referred to in the footnotes by "Jones 1999b."

Citation Formats

In these examples I've used the citation style that I normally use, which is based on author–date Chicago style and is derived from the *Chicago Manual of Style*. The 16th edition of the CMS is current, and information and samples can be found at: http://www.chicagomanualofstyle.org/tools_citationguide.html.

Author–date Chicago style allows for in-text citations instead of footnotes. For example:

> It's clear that Roman adaptability rendered the power of elephants moot. Scipio was ready for them, and Hannibal's elephants, even setting aside the injury they did to the Carthaginians, ended up not causing any real damage to the Romans (Charles and Rhodan 2007, 388).

The idea is the same: after material that comes from a source, refer to that bibliography item and give the page.

Other academic documentation systems, such as Modern Language Association or MLA style, also have in-text citations. (For more on MLA cites you can consult, e.g.,:
http://owl.english.purdue.edu/owl/resource/747/02/.)

I don't care what citation style you use, or whether you use footnotes or in-text cites. What matters is that the cites are there and that you've properly documented the evidence you've collected from primary and secondary sources.

A FINAL WORD

Academic papers aren't about regurgitating facts—especially in history courses. They're about using your interpretive skills to make sense of imperfect evidence, and making an argument that your interpretation is the right one.

That's how history scholarship has worked for hundreds of years. So go out there and do it. Understand the truth. Accumulate the evidence. And convince your reader of something wild and wonderful about the human experience.

APPENDIX: EXAMINING PRIMARY SOURCES

Primary sources are the most direct and most powerful way to connect with people and events of the past. But primary sources must be interpreted, because every source originates from a certain point of view and is intended for a certain audience, and therefore tells only part of the story. Our job is to figure out what part is being told, how it relates to what else we know, and what's being left out.

You should ask yourself these questions each time you encounter a primary source.

1. Who wrote this document, when, and where?

In documents provided for a course, as in a course reader or handout, you will usually be provided this information in the headnote to the source; otherwise it will be in the introduction to the edition you're working from. The who, when, and where provides the context you need to get beyond the document's face value.

2. What type of document is this?

Primary sources come in all types, and which type tells us something about what was going through the author's mind when he or she wrote it. For example, a newspaper article would normally be written to be a concise and informative communications to many readers, while a private diary entry is probably more candid and informal, intended to be seen by few or none, or perhaps intended to be read by the writer's family or descendants. (Although this discussion is framed largely in terms of written documents, all primary sources—artifacts, recordings, graffiti, and so on—can be treated with these same steps.)

3. Who is the intended audience of the document?

Most documents are intended to communicate ideas and viewpoints to a person or a group. Authors tailor their arguments to their target audience, sometimes without realizing it, using their knowledge of the target to elicit the best response. Also, there may be more than one audience: a general writing a military dispatch, for example, might be thinking both of his superiors at headquarters and the general public.

4. What are the main points of the document?

Boil it all down. What is the author ultimately trying to get the audience to understand?

5. Why was this document written?

What do we know about the impetus for this document? What prompted the author to write it?

6. What does it reveal about the society and time period in which it was created?

Bring together what you know from all of the above and try to get at the real meat of what this document tells us—not just about the author, but also about the author's society and his or her relationship to it (was she a part of the mainstream, or a rebel?). One way of looking at this would be to ask yourself whether the same document could have been written 10 years before, or 10 years after. Why not—what changed?

7. What's missing?

What point of view is left out? Was it intentional? How would that change the picture presented by the author?

8. What passage stands out the most?

Which sentence or passage did you react most strongly to—out of admiration, revulsion, or strong agreement or disagreement? Think about what caused that reaction: Was is the content alone, or where you affected by the differences between the author's cultural values and your own?

www.ingramcontent.com/pod-product-compliance
Lightning Source LLC
Chambersburg PA
CBHW070124010626
45794CB00012B/1282